AF359724

Interviews

by

Swami Vivekananda

Interviews
by Swami Vivekananda

Copyright © 2023

All Rights reserved.

No part of this publication may be reproduced, stored in a retrieval system, or transmitted in any form or by any means, electronic, mechanical, photocopying or Otherwise, without the written permission of the publisher.
The author/editor asserts the moral right to be identified as the author/editor of this work.

ISBN: 978-93-59393-42-1

Published by

DOUBLE 9 BOOKS

2/13-B, Ansari Road
Daryaganj, New Delhi – 110002
info@double9books.com
www.double9books.com
Tel. 011-40042856

This book is under public domain

ABOUT THE AUTHOR

Swami Vivekananda was born Narendranath Datta in India on January 12, 1863. He died on July 4, 1902, and was the most important student of the Indian saint Ramakrishna. He was an important part of bringing Vedanta and Yoga to the West. He is also charged with making people more aware of other religions and making Hinduism a major world religion. Vivekananda had a lot of success at the Parliament. In the years that followed, he gave hundreds of lectures across the United States, England, and Europe to spread the main ideas of Hinduism. He also started the Vedanta Society of New York and the Vedanta Society of San Francisco, which is now the Vedanta Society of Northern California. Both of these groups became the basis for Vedanta Societies in the West. Vivekananda was one of the most important philosophers and social reformers in India at the time. He was also one of the most successful and powerful Vedanta missionaries in the West.People now think of him as one of the most important people in modern India and Hinduism. Mahatma Gandhi said that after reading Vivekananda's works, he loved his country a thousand times more.

CONTENTS

Miracles

(The Memphis Commercial, 15th January, 1894)

Asked by the reporter for his impressions of America, he said:

"I have a good impression of this country especially of the American women. I have especially remarked on the absence of poverty in America."

The conversation afterward turned to the subject of religions. Swami Vive Kananda expressed the opinion that the World's Parliament of Religions had been beneficial in that it had done much toward broadening ideas.

"What", asked the reporter, "is the generally accepted view held by those of your faith as to the fate after death of one holding the Christian religion?"

"We believe that if he is a good man he will be saved. Even an atheist, if he is a good man, we believe must be saved. That is our religion. We believe all religions are good, only those who hold them must not quarrel."

Swami Vive Kananda was questioned concerning the truthfulness of the marvelous stories of the performance of wonderful feats of conjuring, levitation, suspended animation, and the like in India. Vive Kananda said:

"We do not believe in miracles at all but that apparently strange things may be accomplished under the operation of natural laws. There is a vast amount of literature in India on these subjects, and the people there have made a study of these things.

"Thought-reading and the foretelling of events are successfully practiced by the Hathayogis.

"As to levitation, I have never seen anyone overcome gravitation and rise by will into the air, but I have seen many who were trying to do so. They read books published on the subject and spend years trying to accomplish the feat. Some of them in their efforts nearly starve themselves and become so thin that if one presses his finger upon their stomachs he can actually feel the spine.

"Some of these Hathayogis live to a great age."

The subject of suspended animation was broached and the Hindu monk told the *Commercial* reporter that he himself had known a man who went into a sealed cave, which was then closed up with a trap door, and remained there for many years without food. There was a decided stir of interest among those who heard this assertion. Vive Kananda entertained not the slightest doubt of the genuineness of this case. He says that in the case of suspended animation, growth is for the time arrested. He says the case of the man in India who was buried with a crop of barley raised over his grave and who was finally taken out still alive is perfectly well authenticated. He thinks the studies which enabled persons to accomplish that feat were suggested by the hibernating animals.

Vive Kananda said that he had never seen the feat which some writers have claimed has been accomplished in India, of throwing a rope into the air and the thrower climbing up the rope and disappearing out of sight in the distant heights.

A lady present when the reporter was interviewing the monk said some one had asked her if he, Vive Kananda, could perform wonderful tricks, and if he had been buried alive as a part of his installation in the Brotherhood. The answer to both questions was a positive negative. "What have those things to do with religion?" he asked. "Do they make a man purer? The Satan of your Bible is powerful, but differs from God in not being pure."

Speaking of the sect of Hathayoga, Vive Kananda said there was one thing, whether a coincidence or not, connected with the initiation of their disciples, which was suggestive of the one passage in the life of Christ. They make their disciples live alone for just forty days.

An Indian Yogi In London

(*The Westminster Gazette, 23rd October, 1895*)

Indian philosophy has in recent years had a deep and growing fascination for many minds, though up to the present time its exponents in this country have been entirely Western in their thought and training, with the result that very little is really known of the deeper mysteries of the Vedanta wisdom, and that little only by a select few. Not many have the courage or the intuition to seek in heavy translations, made greatly in the interests of philologists, for that sublime knowledge which they really reveal to an able exponent brought up in all the traditions of the East.

It was therefore with interest and not without some curiosity, writes a correspondent, that I proceeded to interview an exponent entirely novel to Western people in the person of the Swami Vivekananda, an actual Indian Yogi, who has boldly undertaken to visit the Western world to expound the traditional teaching which has been handed down by ascetics and Yogis through many ages and who In pursuance of this object, delivered a lecture last night in the Princes' Hall.

The Swami Vivekananda is a striking figure with his turban (or mitre-shaped black cloth cap) and his calm but kindly features.

On my inquiring as to the significance, if any, of his name, the Swami said: "Of the name by which I am now known (Swami Vivekananda), the first word is descriptive of a Sannyâsin, or one who formally renounces the world, and the second is the title I assumed — as is customary with all Sannyasins — on my renunciation of the world, it signifies, literally, 'the bliss of discrimination'."

"And what induced you to forsake the ordinary course of the world, Swami?" I asked.

"I had a deep interest in religion and philosophy from my childhood," he replied, "and our books teach renunciation as the highest ideal to which man can aspire. It only needed the meeting with a great Teacher — Ramakrishna Paramahamsa — to kindle in me the final determination to follow the path he himself had trod, as in him I found my highest ideal realised."

"Then did he found a sect, which you now represent?"

"No", replied the Swami quickly. "No, his whole life was spent in breaking down the barriers of sectarianism and dogma. He formed no sect. Quite the reverse. He advocated and strove to establish absolute freedom of thought. He was a great Yogi."

"Then you are connected with no society or sect in this country? Neither Theosophical nor Christian Scientist, nor any other?"

"None whatever!" said the Swami in clear and impressive tones. (His face lights up like that of a child, it is so simple, straightforward and honest.) "My teaching is my own interpretation of our ancient books, in the light which my Master shed upon them. I claim no supernatural authority. Whatever in my teaching may appeal to the highest intelligence and be accepted by thinking men, the adoption of that will be my reward." "All religions", he continued, "have for their object the teaching either of devotion, knowledge, or Yoga, in a concrete form. Now, the philosophy of Vedanta is the abstract science which embraces all these methods, and this it is that I teach, leaving each one to apply it to his own concrete form. I refer each individual to his own experiences, and where reference is made to books, the latter are procurable, and may be studied by each one for himself. Above all, I teach no authority proceeding from hidden beings speaking through visible agents, any more than I claim learning from hidden books or manuscripts. I am the exponent of no occult societies, nor do I believe that good can come of such bodies. Truth stands on its own authority, and truth can bear the light of day."

"Then you do not propose to form any society. Swami?" I suggested.

"None; no society whatever. I teach only the Self hidden in the heart of every individual and common to all. A handful of strong men knowing that Self and living in Its light would revolutionise the world, even today, as has been the case by single strong men before each in his day."

"Have you just arrived from India?" I inquired — for the Swami is suggestive of Eastern suns.

"No," he replied, "I represented the Hindu religion at the Parliament of Religions held at Chicago in 1893. Since then I have been travelling and lecturing in the United States. The American people have proved most interested audiences and sympathetic friends, and my work there has so taken root that I must shortly return to that country."

"And what is your attitude towards the Western religions, Swami?"

"I propound a philosophy which can serve as a basis to every possible religious system in the world, and my attitude towards all of them is one of extreme sympathy — my teaching is antagonistic to none. I direct my attention to the individual, to make him strong, to teach him that he himself is divine, and I call upon men to make themselves conscious of this divinity within. That is really the ideal — conscious or unconscious — of every religion."

"And what shape will your activities take in this country?"

"My hope is to imbue individuals with the teachings to which I have referred, and to encourage them to express these to others in their own way; let them modify them as they will; I do not teach them as dogmas; truth at length must inevitably prevail.

"The actual machinery through which I work is in the hands of one or two friends. On October 22, they have arranged for me to deliver an address to a British audience at Princes' Hall, Piccadilly, at 8-30 p.m. The event is being advertised. The subject will be on the key of my philosophy — 'Self-Knowledge'. Afterwards I am prepared to follow any course that opens — to attend meetings in people's drawing-rooms or elsewhere, to answer letters, or discuss personally. In a mercenary age I may venture to remark that none of my activities are undertaken for a pecuniary reward."

I then took my leave from one of the most original of men that I have had the honour of meeting.

India's Mission

(Sunday Times, London, 1896)

English people are well acquainted with the fact that they send missionaries to India's "coral strands". Indeed, so thoroughly do they obey the behest, "Go ye forth into all the world and preach the Gospel", that none of the chief British sects are behindhand in obedience to the call to spread Christ's teaching. People are not so well aware that India also sends missionaries to England.

By accident, if the term may be allowed, I fell across the Swami Vivekananda in his temporary home at 63 St. George's Road, S. W., and as he did not object to discuss the nature of his work and visit to England, I sought him there and began our talk with an expression of surprise at his assent to my request.

"I got thoroughly used to the interviewer in America. Because it is not the fashion in my country, that is no reason why I should not use means existing in any country I visit, for spreading what I desire to be known! There I was representative of the Hindu religion at the World's Parliament of Religions at Chicago in 1893. The Raja of Mysore and some other friends sent me there. I think I may lay claim to having had some success in America. I had many invitations to other great American cities besides Chicago; my visit was a very long one, for, with the exception of a visit to England last summer, repeated as you see this year, I remained about three years in America. The American civilisation is, in my opinion. a very great one. I find the American mind peculiarly susceptible to new ideas; nothing is rejected because it is new. It is examined on its own merits, and stands or falls by these alone."

"Whereas in England — you mean to imply something?"

"Yes, in England, civilisation is older, it has gathered many accretions as the centuries have rolled on. In particular, you have many prejudices that need to be broken through, and whoever deals with you in ideas must lay this to his account."

"So they say. I gather that you did not found anything like a church or a new religion in America."

"That is true. It is contrary to our principles to multiply organizations, since, in all conscience, there are enough of them. And when organizations are created they need individuals to look after them. Now, those who have made Sannyâsa — that is, renunciation of all worldly position, property, and name — whose aim is to seek spiritual knowledge, cannot undertake this work, which is, besides, in other hands."

"Is your teaching a system of comparative religion?"

"It might convey a more definite idea to call it the kernel of all forms of religion, stripping from them the non-essential, and laying stress on that which is the real basis. I am a disciple of Ramakrishna Paramahamsa, a perfect Sannyâsin whose influence and ideas I fell under. This great Sannyasin never assumed the negative or critical attitude towards other religions, but showed their positive side — how they could be carried into life and practiced. To fight, to assume the antagonistic attitude, is the exact contrary of his teaching, which dwells on the truth that the world is moved by love. You know that the Hindu religion never persecutes. It is the land where all sects may live in peace and amity. The Mohammedans brought murder and slaughter in their train, but until their arrival peace prevailed. Thus the Jains, who do not believe in a God and who regard such belief as a delusion, were tolerated, and still are there today. India sets the example of real strength, that is meekness. Dash, pluck, fight, all these things are weakness."

"It sounds very like Tolstoy's doctrine; it may do for individuals, though personally I doubt it. But how will it answer for nations?"

"Admirably for them also. It was India's Karma, her fate, to be conquered, and in her turn, to conquer her conqueror. She has already done so with her Mohammedan victors: Educated Mohammedans are Sufis, scarcely to be distinguished from Hindus. Hindu thought has permeated their civilisation; they assumed the position of learners. The great Akbar, the Mogul Emperor, was practically a Hindu. And England will be conquered in her turn. Today she has the sword, but it is worse than useless in the world of ideas. You know what Schopenhauer said of Indian thought. He foretold that its influence would be as momentous in Europe, when it became well known, as the revival of Greek and Latin; culture after the Dark Ages."

"Excuse me saying that there do not seem many signs; of it just now."

"Perhaps not", said the Swami, gravely. "I dare say a good many people saw no signs of the old Renaissance and did not know it was there, even after it had come. But there is a great movement, which can be discerned by those who know the signs of the times. Oriental research has of recent years made great progress. At present it is in the hands of scholars, and it seems dry and heavy in the work they have achieved. But gradually the light of comprehension will break"

"And India is to be the great conqueror of the future? Yet she does not send out many missionaries to preach her ideas. I presume she will wait until the world comes to her feet?"

"India was once a great missionary power. Hundreds' of years before England was converted to Christianity, Buddha sent out missionaries to convert the world of Asia to his doctrine. The world of thought is being converted. We are only at the beginning as yet. The number of those who decline to adopt any special form of religion is greatly increasing, and this movement is among the educated classes. In a recent American census, a large number of persons declined to class themselves as belonging to any form of religion. All religions are different expressions of the same truth; all march on or die out. They are the radii of the same truth, the expression that variety of minds requires."

"Now we are getting near it. What is that central truth ?"

"The Divine within; every being, however degraded, is the expression of the Divine. The Divinity becomes covered, hidden from view. I call to mind an incident of the Indian Mutiny. A Swami, who for years had fulfilled a vow of eternal silence, was stabbed by a Mohammedan. They dragged the murderer before his victim and cried out, 'Speak the word, Swami, and he shall die.' After many years of silence, he broke it to say with his last breath: 'My children, you are all mistaken. That man is God Himself.' The great lesson is, that unity is behind all. Call it God, Love, Spirit. Allah, Jehovah — it is the same unity that animates all life from the lowest animal to the noblest man. Picture to yourself an ocean ice-bound, pierced with many different holes. Each of these is a soul, a man, emancipated according to his degree of intelligence, essaying to break through the ice."

"I think I see one difference between the wisdom of the East and that of the West. You aim at producing very perfect individuals by Sannyasa, concentration, and so forth. Now the ideal of the West seems to be the perfecting of the social state; and so we work at political and social questions, since we think that the permanence of our civilisation depends upon the well-being of the people."

"But the basis of all systems, social or political," said the Swami with great earnestness, "rests upon the goodness of men. No nation is great or good because Parliament enacts this or that, but because its men are great and good. I have visited China which had the most admirable organisation of all nations. Yet today China is like a disorganised mob, because her men are not equal to the system contrived in the olden days. Religion goes to the root of the matter. If it is right, all is right."

"It sounds just a little vague and remote from practical life, that the Divine is within everything but covered. One can't be looking for it all the time."

"People often work for the same ends but fail to recognise the fact. One must admit that law, government, politics are phases not final in any way. There is a goal beyond them where law is not needed. And by the way, the very word Sannyasin means the divine outlaw, one might say, divine nihilist, but that miscomprehension pursues those that use such a word. All great Masters teach the same thing. Christ saw that the basis is not law, that morality and purity are the only strength. As for your statement that the East aims at higher self-development and the West at the perfecting of the social state, you do not of course forget that there is an apparent Self and a real Self."

"The inference, of course, being that we work for the apparent, you for the real?"

"The mind works through various stages to attain its fuller development. First, it lays hold of the concrete, and only gradually deals with abstractions. Look, too, how the idea of universal brotherhood is reached. First it is grasped as brotherhood within a sect — hard, narrow, and exclusive. Step by step we reach broad generalizations and the world of abstract ideas."

"So you think that those sects, of which we English are so fond, will die out. You know what the Frenchman said, 'England, the land of a thousand sects and but one sauce'."

"I am sure that they are bound to disappear. Their existence is founded on non-essentials; the essential part of them will remain and be built up into another edifice. You know the old saying that it is good to be born in a church, but not to die in it."

"Perhaps you will say how your work is progressing in England?"

"Slowly, for the reasons I have already named. When you deal with roots and foundations, all real progress must be slow. Of course, I need not say that these ideas are bound to spread by one means or another, and to many of us the right moment for their dissemination seems now to have come."

Then I listened to an explanation of how work is carried on. Like many an old doctrine, this new one is offered without money and without price, depending entirely upon the voluntary efforts of those who embrace it.

The Swami is a picturesque figure in his Eastern dress. His simple and cordial manner, savouring of anything but the popular idea of asceticism, an unusual command of English and great conversational powers add not a little to an interesting personality. . . . His vow of Sannyasa implies renunciation of position, property, and name, as well as the persistent search for spiritual knowledge.

India And England

(India, London, 1896)

During the London season, Swami Vivekananda has been teaching and lecturing to considerable numbers of people who have been attracted by his doctrine and philosophy. Most English people fancy that England has the practical monopoly of missionary enterprise, almost unbroken save for a small effort on the part of France. I therefore sought the Swami in his temporary home in South Belgravia to enquire what message India could possibly send to England, apart from the remonstrances she has too often had to make on the subject of home charges, judicial and executive functions combined in one person, the settlement of expenses connected with Sudanese and other expeditions.

"It is no new thing", said the Swami composedly, "that India should send forth missionaries. She used to do so under the Emperor Asoka, in the days when the Buddhist faith was young, when she had something to teach the surrounding nation."

"Well, might one ask why she ever ceased doing so, and why she has now begun again?"

"She ceased because she grew selfish, forgot the principle that nations and individuals alike subsist and prosper by a system of give and take. Her mission to the world has always been the same. It is spiritual, the realm of introspective thought has been hers through all the ages; abstract science, metaphysics, logic, are her special domain. In reality, my mission to England is an outcome of England's to India. It has been hers to conquer, to govern, to use her knowledge of physical science to her advantage and ours. In trying to sum up India's contribution to the world, I am reminded of a Sanskrit and an English idiom. When you say a man dies, your phrase is, 'He gave up the ghost', whereas we say, 'He gave up the body'. Similarly, you more than imply that the body is the chief part of man by saying it possesses a soul. Whereas we say a man is a soul and possesses a body. These are but small ripples on the surface, yet they show the current of your national thought. I should like to remind you how Schopenhauer predicted that the influence of Indian philosophy upon Europe would be as momentous when it became well known as was the revival of Greek and Latin learning at the close of the

Dark Ages. Oriental research is making great progress; a new world of ideas is opening to the seeker after truth."

"And is India finally to conquer her conquerors?"

"Yes, in the world of ideas. England has the sword, the material world, as our Mohammedan conquerors had before her. Yet Akbar the Great became practically a Hindu; educated Mohammedans, the Sufis, are hardly to be distinguished from the Hindus; they do not eat beef, and in other ways conform to our usages. Their thought has become permeated by ours."

"So, that is the fate you foresee for the lordly Sahib? Just at this moment he seems to be a long way off it."

"No, it is not so remote as you imply. In the world of religious ideas, the Hindu and the Englishman have much in common, and there is proof of the same thing among other religious communities. Where the English ruler or civil servant has had any knowledge of India's literature, especially her philosophy, there exists the ground of a common sympathy, a territory constantly widening. It is not too much to say that only ignorance is the cause of that exclusive — sometimes even contemptuous — attitude assumed by some."

"Yes, it is the measure of folly. Will you say why you went to America rather than to England on your mission?"

"That was a mere accident — a result of the World's Parliament of Religions being held in Chicago at the time of the World's Fair, instead of in London, as it ought to have been. The Raja of Mysore and some other friends sent me to America as the Hindu representative. I stayed there three years, with the exception of last summer and this summer, when I came to lecture in London. The Americans are a great people, with a future before them. I admire them very much, and found many kind friends among them. They are less prejudiced than the English, more ready to weigh end examine anew idea, to value it in spite of its newness. They are most hospitable too; far less time is lost in showing one's credentials, as it were. You travel in America, as I did, from city to city, always lecturing among friends. I saw Boston, New York, Philadelphia, Baltimore, Washington, Des Moines, Memphis, and numbers of other places."

"And leaving disciples in each of them?"

"Yes, disciples, but not organizations. That is no part of my work. Of these there are enough in all conscience. Organisations need men to manage them; they must seek power, money, influence. Often they struggle for domination, and even fight."

"Could the gist of this mission of yours be summed up in a few words? Is it comparative religion you want to preach?"

"It is really the philosophy of religion, the kernel of all its outward forms. All forms of religion have an essential and a non-essential part. If we strip from them the latter, there remains the real basis of all religion, which all forms of religion possess in common. Unity is behind them all. We may call it God, Allah, Jehovah, the Spirit, Love; it is the same unity that animates all life, from its lowest form to its noblest manifestation in man. It is on this unity that we need to lay stress, whereas in the West, and indeed everywhere, it is on the non-essential that men are apt to lay stress. They will fight and kill each other for these forms, to make their fellows conform. Seeing that the essential is love of God and love of man, this is curious, to say the least."

"I suppose a Hindu could never persecute."

"He never yet has done so; he is the most tolerant of all the races of men. Considering how profoundly religious he is, one might have thought that he would persecute those who believe in no God. The Jains regard such belief as sheer delusion, yet no Jain has ever been persecuted. In India the Mohammedans were the first who ever took the sword."

"What progress does the doctrine of essential unity make in England? Here we have a thousand sects."

"They must gradually disappear as liberty and knowledge increase. They are founded on the nonessential, which by the nature of things cannot survive. The sects have served their purpose, which was that of an exclusive brotherhood on lines comprehended by those within it. Gradually we reach the idea of universal brotherhood by flinging down the walls of partition which separate such aggregations of individuals. In England the work proceeds slowly, possibly because the time is not yet ripe for it; but all the same, it makes progress. Let me call your attention to the similar work that England is engaged upon in India. Modern caste distinction is a barrier to India's progress. It narrows, restricts, separates. It will crumble before the advance of ideas.

"Yet some Englishmen, and they are not the least sympathetic to India nor the most ignorant of her history, regard caste as in the main beneficent. One may easily be too much Europeanised. You yourself condemn many of our ideals as materialistic."

"True. No reasonable person aims at assimilating India to England; the body is made by the thought that lies behind it. The body politic is thus the expression of national thought, and in India, of thousands of years of thought. To Europeanise India is therefore an impossible and foolish task: the elements of progress were always actively present in India. As soon as a peaceful government was there, these have always shown themselves. From the time of the Upanishads down to the present day, nearly all our great Teachers have wanted to break through the barriers of caste, i.e. caste in its degenerate state, not the original system. What little good you see in the present caste clings to it from the original caste, which was the most glorious social institution. Buddha tried to re-establish caste in its original form. At every period of India's awakening, there have always been great efforts made to break down caste. But it must always be *we* who build up a new India as an effect and continuation of her past, assimilating helpful foreign ideas wherever they may be found. Never can it be they; growth must proceed from within. All that England can do is to help India to work out her own salvation. All progress at the dictation of another, whose hand is at India's throat, is valueless in my opinion. The highest work can only degenerate when slave-labour produces it."

"Have you given any attention to the Indian National Congress movement?"

"I cannot claim to have given much; my work is in another part of the field. But I regard the movement as significant, and heartily wish it success. A nation is being made out of India's different races. I sometimes think they are no less various than the different peoples of Europe. In the past, Europe has struggled for Indian trade, a trade which has played a tremendous part in the civilisation of the world; its acquisition might almost be called a turning-point in the history of humanity. We see the Dutch, Portuguese, French, and English contending for it in succession. The discovery of America may be traced to the indemnification the Venetians sought in the far distant West for the loss they suffered in the East."

"Where will it end?"

"It will certainly end in the working out of India's homogeneity, in her acquiring what we may call democratic ideas. Intelligence must not remain the monopoly of the cultured few; it will be disseminated from higher to lower classes. Education is coming, and compulsory education will follow. The immense power of our people for work must be utilised. India's potentialities are great and will be called forth"

"Has any nation ever been great without being a great military power?"

"Yes," said the Swami without a moment's hesitation, "China has. Amongst other countries, I have travelled in China and Japan. Today, China is like a disorganised mob; but in the heyday of her greatness she possessed the most admirable organisation any nation has yet known Many of the devices and methods we term modern were practiced by the Chinese for hundreds and even thousands of years. Take competitive examination as an illustration."

"Why did she become disorganized?"

"Because she could not produce men equal to the system. You have the saying that men cannot be made virtuous by an Act of Parliament; the Chinese experienced it before you. And that is why religion is of deeper importance than politics, since it goes to the root, and deals with the essential of conduct."

"Is India conscious of the awakening that you allude to?"

"Perfectly conscious. The world perhaps sees it chiefly in the Congress movement and in the field of social reform; but the awakening is quite as real in religion, though it works more silently."

"The West and East have such different ideals of life. Ours seems to be the perfecting of the social state. Whilst we are busy seeing to these matters, Orientals are meditating on abstractions. Here has Parliament been discussing the payment of the Indian army in the Sudan. All the respectable section of the Conservative press has made a loud outcry against the unjust decision of the Government, whereas you probably think the whole affair not worth attention."

"But you are quite wrong", said the Swami, taking the paper and running his eyes over extracts from the Conservative Journals. "My sympathies in this matter are naturally with my country. Yet it reminds one of the old Sanskrit proverb: 'You have sold the elephant, why quarrel over the goad?' India always pays. The quarrels of politicians are very curious. It will take ages to bring religion into politics."

"One ought to make the effort very soon all the same."

"Yes, it is worth one's while to plant an idea in the heart of this great London, surely the greatest governing machine that has ever been set in motion. I often watch it working, the power and perfection with which the minutest vein is reached, its wonderful system of circulation and distribution. It helps one to realise how great is the Empire and how great its task. And with all the rest, it distributes thought. It would be worth a man's while to place some ideas in the heart of this great machine, so that they might circulate to the remotest part."

The Swami is a man of distinguished appearance. Tall, broad, with fine features enhanced by his picturesque Eastern dress, his personality is very striking. By birth, he is a Bengali, and by education, a graduate of the Calcutta University. His gifts as an orator are high. He can speak for an hour and a half without a note or the slightest pause for a word.

C. S. B.

Indian Missionary's Mission To England

(The Echo, London, 1896)

. . . I presume that in his own country the Swami would live under a tree, or at most in the precincts of a temple, his head shaved, dressed in the costume of his country. But these things are not done in London, so that I found the Swami located much like other people, and, save that he wears a long coat of a dark orange shade, dressed like other mortals likewise. He laughingly related that his dress, especially when he wears a turban, does not commend itself to the London street arab, whose observations are scarcely worth repeating. I began by asking the Indian Yogi to spell his name very slowly. . . .

"Do you think that nowadays people are laying much stress on the non-essential?"

"I think so among the backward nations, and among the less cultured portion of the civilised people of the West. Your question implies that among the cultured and the wealthy, matters are on a different footing. So they are; the wealthy are either immersed in the enjoyment of health or grubbing for more. They, and a large section of the busy people, say of religion that it is rot, stuff, nonsense, and they honestly think so The only religion that is fashionable is patriotism and Mrs. Grundy. People merely go to church when they are marrying or burying somebody."

"Will your message take them oftener to church?"

"I scarcely think it will. Since I have nothing whatever to do with ritual or dogma; my mission is to show that religion is everything and in everything. . . . And what can we say of the system here in England? Everything goes to show that Socialism or some form of rule by the people, call it what you will, is coming on the boards. The people will certainly want the satisfaction of their material needs, less work, no oppression, no war, more food. What guarantee have we that this or any civilisation will last, unless it is based on religion, on the goodness of man? Depend on it, religion goes to the root of the matter. If it is right, all is right."

"It must be difficult to get the essential, the metaphysical, part of religion into the minds of the people. It is remote from their thoughts and manner of life."

"In all religions we travel from a lesser to a higher truth, never from error to truth. There is a Oneness behind all creation, but minds are very various. 'That which exists is One, sages call It variously.' What I mean is that one progresses from a smaller to a greater truth. The worst religions are only bad readings of the froth. One gets to understand bit by bit. Even devil-worship is but a perverted reading of the ever-true and immutable Brahman. Other phases have more or less of the truth in them. No form of religion possesses it entirely."

"May one ask if you originated this religion you have come to preach to England?"

"Certainly not. I am a pupil of a great Indian sage, Ramakrishna Paramahamsa. He was not what one might call a very learned man, as some of our sages are, but a very holy one, deeply imbued with the spirit of the Vedanta philosophy. When I say philosophy, I hardly know whether I ought not to say religion, for it is really both. You must read Professor Max Müller's account of my Master in a recent number of the *Nineteenth Century*. Ramakrishna was born in the Hooghly district in 1836 and died in 1886. He produced a deep effect on the life of Keshab Chandra Sen and others. By discipline of the body and subduing of the mind he obtained a wonderful insight into the spiritual world. His face was distinguished by a childlike tenderness, profound humility, and remarkable sweetness of expression. No one could look upon it unmoved."

"Then your teaching is derived from the Vedas?"

"Yes, Vedanta means the end of the Vedas, the third section or Upanishads, containing the ripened ideas which we find more as germs in the earlier portion. The most ancient portion of the Vedas is the Samhitâ, which is in very archaic Sanskrit, only to be understood by the aid of a very old dictionary, the Nirukta of Yâska."

"I fear that we English have rather the idea that India has much to learn from us; the average man is pretty ignorant as to what may be learnt from India."

"That is so, but the world of scholars know well how much is to be learnt and how important the lesson. You would not find Max Müller, Monier Williams, Sir William Hunter, or German Oriental scholars making light of Indian abstract science."

. . . The Swami gives his lecture at 39 Victoria Street. All are made welcome, and as in ancient apostolic times, the new teaching is without money and without price. The Indian missionary is a mall of exceptionally fine physique; his command of English can only be described as perfect.

C. S. B.

With The Swami Vivekananda At Madura

(The Hindu, Madras, February, 1897)

Q. — The theory that the universe is false seems to be understood in the following senses: (a) the sense in which the duration of perishing forms and names is infinitesimally small with reference to eternity; (b) the sense in which the period between any two Pralayas (involution of the universe) is infinitesimally small with reference to eternity; (c) the sense in which the universe is ultimately false though it has an apparent reality at present, depending upon one sort of consciousness, in the same way as the idea of silver superimposed on a shell or that of a serpent on a rope, is true for the time being, and, in effect, is dependent upon a particular condition of mind; (d) the sense in which the universe is a phantom just like the son of a barren woman or like the horns of a hare.

In which of these senses is the theory understood in the Advaita philosophy?

A. — There are many classes of Advaitists and each has understood the theory in one or the other sense. Shankara taught the theory in the sense (c), and it is his teaching that the universe, as it appears, is real for all purposes for every one in his present consciousness, but it vanishes when the consciousness assumes a higher form. You see the trunk of a tree standing before you, and you mistake it for a ghost. The idea of a ghost is for the time being real, for it works on your mind and produces the same result upon it as if it were a ghost. As soon as you discover it to be a stump, the idea of the ghost disappears. The idea of a stump and that of the ghost cannot co-exist, and when one is present, the other is absent.

Q. — Is not the sense (d) also adopted in some of the writings of Shankara?

A. — No. Some other men who, by mistake, carried Shankara's notion to an extreme have adopted the sense (d) in their writing. The senses (a) and (b) are peculiar to the writings of some other classes of Advaita philosophers but never received Shankara's sanction.

Q. — What is the cause of the apparent reality?

A. — What is the cause of your mistaking a stump for a ghost? The universe is the same, in fact, but it is your mind that creates various conditions for it.

Q. — What is the true meaning of the statement that the Vedas are beginningless and eternal? Does it refer to the Vedic utterances or the statements contained in the Vedas? If it refers to the truth involved in such statements, are not the sciences, such as Logic, Geometry, Chemistry, etc., equally beginningless and eternal, for they contain an everlasting truth?

A. — There was a time when the Vedas themselves were considered eternal in the sense in which the divine truths contained therein were changeless and permanent and were only revealed to man. At a subsequent time, it appears that the utterance of the Vedic hymns with the knowledge of its meaning was important, and it was held that the hymns themselves must have had a divine origin. At a still later period the meaning of the hymns showed that many of them could not be of divine origin, because they inculcated upon mankind performance of various unholy acts, such as torturing animals, and we can also find many ridiculous stories in the Vedas. The correct meaning of the statement "The Vedas are beginningless and eternal" is that the law or truth revealed by them to man is permanent and changeless. Logic, Geometry, Chemistry, etc., reveal also a law or truth which is permanent and changeless, and in that sense they are also beginningless and eternal. But no truth or law is absent from the Vedas, and I ask any one of you to point out to me any truth which is not treated of in them.

Q. — What is the notion of Mukti, according to the Advaita philosophy, or in other words, is it a conscious state? Is there any difference between the Mukti of the Advaitism and the Buddhistic Nirvâna?

A. — There is a consciousness in Mukti, which we call superconsciousness. It differs from your present consciousness. It is illogical to say that there is no consciousness in Mukti. The consciousness is of three sorts — the dull, mediocre, and intense — as is the case of light. When vibration is intense, the brilliancy is so very powerful as to dazzle the sight itself and in effect is as ineffectual as the dullest of lights. The Buddhistic Nirvana must have the same degree of consciousness whatever the Buddhists may say. Our definition of Mukti is affirmative in its nature, while the Buddhistic Nirvana has a negative definition.

Q. — Why should the unconditioned Brahman choose to assume a condition for the purpose of manifestation of the world's creation?

A. — The question itself is most illogical. Brahman is *Avângmanasogocharam,* meaning that which is incapable of being grasped by word and mind. Whatever lies beyond the region of space, time and causation cannot be conceived by the human mind, and the function of logic and enquiry lies only within the region of space, time, and causation. While that is so, it is a vain attempt to question about what lies beyond the possibilities of human conception.

Q. — Here and there attempts are made to import into the Purânas hidden ideas which are said to have been allegorically represented. Sometimes it is said that the Puranas need not contain any historical truth, but are mere representations of the highest ideals illustrated with fictitious characters. Take for instance, Vishnupurâna, Râmâyana, or Bhârata. Do they contain historical veracity or are they mere allegorical representations of metaphysical truths, or are they representations of the highest ideals for the conduct of humanity, or are they mere epic poems such as those of Homer?

A. — Some historical truth is the nucleus of every Purana. The object of the Puranas is to teach mankind the sublime truth in various forms; and even if they do not contain any historical truth, they form a great authority for us in respect of the highest truth which they inculcate. Take the Râmâyana, for illustration, and for viewing it as an authority on building character, it is not even necessary that one like Rama should have ever lived. The sublimity of the law propounded by Ramayana or Bharata does not depend upon the truth of any personality like Rama or Krishna, and one can even hold that such personages never lived, and at the same time take those writings as high authorities in respect of the grand ideas which they place before mankind. Our philosophy does not depend upon any personality for its truth. Thus Krishna did not teach anything new or original to the world, nor does Ramayana profess anything which is not contained in the Scriptures. It is to be noted that Christianity cannot stand without Christ, Mohammedanism without Mohammed, and Buddhism without Buddha, but Hinduism stands independent of any man, and for the purpose of estimating the philosophical truth contained in any Purana, we need not consider the question whether the personages treated of therein were really material men or were fictitious characters. The object of the Puranas was the education of mankind, and the sages who constructed them contrived to find some historical personages and to superimpose upon them all the best or worst qualities just as they wanted to, and laid down the rules of morals for the conduct of mankind. Is it necessary that a demon with ten heads (Dashamukha) should have actually lived as stated in the Ramayana? It is the representation of some truth which deserves to be studied, apart from the question whether Dashamukha was a real or fictitious character. You can now depict Krishna in a still more attractive manner, and the description depends upon the sublimity of your ideal, but there stands the grand philosophy contained in the Puranas.

Q. — Is it possible for a man, if he were an adept, to remember the events connected with his past incarnations? The physiological brain, which he owned in his previous incarnation, and in which the impressions of his experience were stored, is no longer present. In this birth he is endowed with a new physiological brain, and while that is so, how is it possible for the present brain to get at the impressions received by another apparatus which is not existence at present?

Swami — What do you mean by an adept?

Correspondent — One that has developed the hidden powers of his nature.

Swami — I cannot understand how the hidden powers can be developed. I know what you mean, but I should always desire that the expressions used are precise and accurate. You may say that the powers hidden are uncovered. It is possible for those that have uncovered the hidden powers of their nature to remember the incidents connected with their past incarnations, for their present brain had its Bija (seed) in the Sukshma man after death.

Q. — Does the spirit of Hinduism permit the proselytism of strangers into it? And can a Brâhmin listen to the exposition of philosophy made by a Chandâla?

A. — Proselytism is tolerated by Hinduism. Any man, whether he be a Shudra or Chandala, can expound philosophy even to a Brahmin. The truth can be learnt from the lowest individual, no matter to what caste or creed he belongs.

Here the Swami quoted Sanskrit verses of high authority in support of his position.

The discourse ended, as the time appointed in the programme for his visiting the Temple had already arrived. He accordingly took leave of the gentlemen present and proceeded to visit the Temple.

The Abroad And The Problems At Home

(The Hindu, Madras, February, 1897)

Our representative met the Swami Vivekananda in the train at the Chingleput Station and travelled with him to Madras. The following is the report of the interview:

"What made you go to America, Swamiji?"

"Rather a serious question to answer in brief. I can only answer it partly now. Because I travelled all over India, I wanted to go over to other countries. I went to America by the Far East."

"What did you see in Japan, and is there any chance of India following in the progressive steps of Japan?"

"None whatever, until all the three hundred millions of India combine together as a whole nation. The world has never seen such a patriotic and artistic race as the Japanese, and one special feature about them is this that while in Europe and elsewhere Art generally goes with dirt, Japanese Art is Art *plus* absolute cleanliness. I would wish that every one of our young men could visit Japan once at least in his lifetime. It is very easy to go there. The Japanese think that everything Hindu is great and believe that India is a holy land. Japanese Buddhism is entirely different from what you see in Ceylon. It is the same as Vedanta. It is positive and theistic Buddhism, not the negative atheistic Buddhism of Ceylon.

"What is the key to Japan's sudden greatness?"

"The faith of the Japanese in themselves, and their love for their country. When you have men who are ready to sacrifice their everything for their country, sincere to the backbone — when such men arise, India will become great in every respect. It is the men that make the country! What is there in the country? If you catch the social morality and the political morality of the Japanese, you will be as great as they are. The Japanese are ready to sacrifice everything for their country, and they have become a great people. But you are not; you cannot be, you sacrifice everything only for your own families and possessions."

"Is it your wish that India should become like Japan?"

"Decidedly not. India should continue to be what she is. How could India ever become like Japan, or any nation for the matter of that? In each nation, as in music, there is a main note, a central theme, upon which all others turn. Each nation has a theme: everything else is secondary. India's theme is religion. Social reform and everything else are secondary. Therefore India cannot be like Japan. It is said that when 'the heart breaks', then the flow of thought comes. India's heart must break, and the flow of spirituality will come out. India is India. We are not like the Japanese, we are Hindus. India's very atmosphere is soothing. I have been working incessantly here, and amidst this work I am getting rest. It is only from spiritual work that we can get rest in India. If your work is material here, you die of — diabetes!"

"So much for Japan. What was your first experience of America, Swamiji?"

"From first to last it was very good. With the exception of the missionaries and 'Church-women' the Americans are most hospitable, kind-hearted, generous, and good-natured."

"Who are these 'Church-women' that you speak of, Swamiji?"

"When a woman tries her best to find a husband, she goes to all the fashionable seaside resorts and tries all sorts of tricks to catch a man. When she fails in her attempts, she becomes, what they call in America, an 'old maid', and joins the Church. Some of them become very 'Churchy'. These 'Church-women' are awful fanatics. They are under the thumb of the priests there. Between them and the priests they make hell of earth and make a mess of religion. With the exception of these, the Americans are a very good people. They loved me, and I love them a great deal. I felt as if I was one of them."

"What is your idea about the results of the Parliament of Religions?"

"The Parliament of Religions, as it seems to me, was intended for a 'heathen show' before the world: but it turned out that the heathens had the upper hand and made it a Christian show all around. So the Parliament of Religions was a failure from the Christian standpoint, seeing that the Roman Catholics, who were the organisers of that Parliament, are, when there is a talk of another Parliament at Paris, now steadily opposing it. But the Chicago Parliament was a tremendous success for India and Indian thought. It helped on the tide of Vedanta, which is flooding the world. The American people — of course, *minus* the fanatical priests and Church-women — are very glad of the results of the Parliament."

"What prospects have you, Swamiji, for the spread of your mission in England?"

"There is every prospect. Before many years elapse a vast majority of the English people will be Vedantins. There is a greater prospect of this in England than there is in America. You see, Americans make a fanfaronade of everything, which is not the case with Englishmen. Even Christians cannot understand their New Testament, without understanding the Vedanta. The Vedanta is the rationale of all religions. Without the Vedanta every religion is superstition; with it everything becomes religion."

"What is the special trait you noticed in the English character?"

"The Englishman goes to practical work as soon as he believes in something. He has tremendous energy for practical work. There is in the whole world no human being superior to the English gentleman or lady. That is really the reason of my faith in them. John Bull is rather a thick-headed gentleman to deal with. You must push and push an idea till it reaches his brain, but once there, it does not get out. In England, there was not one missionary or anybody who said anything against me; not one who tried to make a scandal about me. To my astonishment, many of my friends belong to the Church of England. I learn, these missionaries do not come from the higher classes in England. Caste is as rigorous there as it is here, and the English churchmen belong to the class of gentlemen. They may differ in opinion from you, but that is no bar to their being friends with you; therefore, I would give a word of advice to my countrymen, which is, not to take notice of the vituperative missionaries, now that I have known that they are. We have 'sized' them, as the Americans say. Non-recognition is the only attitude to assume towards them."

"Will you kindly enlighten me, Swamiji, on the Social Reform movements in America and England?"

"Yes. All the social upheavalists, at least the leaders of them, are trying to find that all their communistic or equalising theories must have a spiritual basis, and that spiritual basis is in the Vedanta only. I have been told by several leaders, who used to attend my lectures, that they required the Vedanta as the basis of the new order of things."

"What are your views with regard to the Indian masses?"

"Oh, we are awfully poor, and our masses are very ignorant about secular things. Our masses are very good because poverty here is not a crime. Our masses are not violent. Many times I was near being mobbed in America and England, only on account of my dress. But I never heard of such a thing in India as a man being mobbed because of peculiar dress. In every other respect, our masses are much more civilised than the European masses."

"What will you propose for the improvement of our masses?"

"We have to give them secular education. We have to follow the plan laid down by our ancestors, that is, to bring all the ideals slowly down among the masses. Raise them slowly up, raise them to equality. Impart even secular knowledge through religion."

"But do you think, Swamiji, it is a task that can be easily accomplished?"

"It will, of course, have gradually to be worked out. But if there are enough self-sacrificing young fellows, who, I hope, will work with me, it can be done tomorrow. It all depends upon the zeal and the self-sacrifice brought to the task."

"But if the present degraded condition is due to their past Karma, Swamiji, how do you think they could get out of it easily, and how do you propose to help them?"

The Swamiji readily answered "Karma is the eternal assertion of human freedom. If we can bring ourselves down by our Karma, surely it is in our power to raise ourselves by it. The masses, besides, have not brought themselves down altogether by their own Karma. So we should give them better environments to work in. I do not propose any levelling of castes. Caste is a very good thing. Caste is the plan we want to follow. What caste really is, not one in a million understands. There is no country in the world without caste. In India, from caste we reach to the point where there is no caste. Caste is based throughout on that principle. The plan in India is to make everybody a Brahmin, the Brahmin being the ideal of humanity. If you read the history of India you will find that attempts have always been made to raise the lower classes. Many are the classes that have been raised. Many more will follow till the whole will become Brahmin. That is the plan. We have only to raise them without bringing down anybody. And this has mostly to be done by the Brahmins themselves, because it is the duty of every aristocracy to dig its own grave; and the sooner it does so, the better for all. No time should be lost. Indian caste is better than the caste which prevails in Europe or America. I do not say it is absolutely good. Where would you be if there were no caste? Where would be your learning and other things, if there were no caste? There would be nothing left for the Europeans to study if caste had never existed! The Mohammedans would have smashed everything to pieces. Where do you find the Indian society standing still? It is always on the move. Sometimes, as in the times of foreign invasions, the movement has been slow, at other times quicker. This is what I say to my countrymen. I do not condemn them. I look into their past. I find that under the circumstances no nation could do more glorious work. I tell them that they have done well. I only ask them to do better."

"What are your views, Swamiji, in regard to the relation of caste to rituals?"

"Caste is continually changing, rituals are continually changing, so are forms. It is the substance, the principle, that does not change. It is in the Vedas that we have to study our religion. With the exception of the Vedas every book must change. The authority of the Vedas is for all time to come; the authority of every one of our other books is for the time being. For instance; one Smriti is powerful for one age, another for another age. Great prophets are always coming and pointing the way to work. Some prophets worked for the lower classes, others like Madhva gave to women the right to study the Vedas. Caste should not go; but should only be readjusted occasionally. Within the old structure is to be found life enough for the building of two hundred thousand new ones. It is sheer nonsense to desire the abolition of caste. The new method is — evolution of the old."

"Do not Hindus stand in need of social reform?"

"We do stand in need of social reform. At times great men would evolve new ideas of progress, and kings would give them the sanction of law. Thus social improvements had been in the past made in India, and in modern times to effect such progressive reforms, we will have first to build up such an authoritative power. Kings having gone, the power is the people's. We have, therefore, to wait till the people are educated, till they understand their needs and are ready and able to solve their problems. The tyranny of the minority is the worst tyranny in the world. Therefore, instead of frittering away our energies on ideal reforms, which will never become practical, we had better go to the root of the evil and make a legislative body, that is to say, educate our people, so that they may be able to solve their own problems. Until that is done all these ideal reforms will remain ideals only. The new order of things is the salvation of the people by the people, and it takes time to make it workable, especially in India, which has always in the past been governed by kings."

"Do you think Hindu society can successfully adopt European social laws?"

"No, not wholly. I would say, the combination of the Greek mind represented by the external European energy added to the Hindu spirituality would be an ideal society for India. For instance, it is absolutely necessary for you, instead of frittering away your energy and often talking of idle nonsense, to learn from the Englishman the idea of prompt obedience to leaders, the absence of jealousy, the indomitable perseverance and the undying faith in himself. As soon as he selects a leader for a work, the Englishman sticks to him through thick and thin and obeys him. Here in India, everybody wants to become a leader, and there is nobody to obey. Everyone should learn to obey before he can command. There is no end to our jealousies; and the more important the Hindu, the more jealous he is. Until this absence of jealousy and obedience to leaders are learnt by the Hindu, there will be no power of organization. We shall have to remain the hopelessly confused mob that we are now, hoping and doing nothing. India has to learn from Europe the conquest of external nature, and Europe has to learn from India the conquest of internal nature. Then there will be neither Hindus nor Europeans — there will be the ideal humanity which has conquered both the natures, the external and the internal. We have developed one phase of humanity, and they another. It is the union of the two that is wanted. The word freedom which is the watchword of our religion really means freedom physically, mentally, and spiritually."

"What relation, Swamiji, does ritual bear to religion?"

"Rituals are the kindergarten of religion. They are absolutely necessary for the world as it is now; only we shall have to give people newer and fresher rituals. A party of thinkers must undertake to do this. Old rituals must be rejected and new ones substituted."

"Then you advocate the abolition of rituals, don't you?"

"No, my watchword is construction, not destruction. Out of the existing rituals, new ones will have to be evolved. There is infinite power of development in everything; that is my belief. One atom has the power of the whole universe at its back. All along, in the history of the Hindu race, there never was any attempt at destruction, only construction. One sect wanted to destroy, and they were thrown out of India: They were the Buddhists. We have had a host of reformers — Shankara, Râmânuja, Madhva, and Chaitanya. These were great reformers, who always were constructive and built according to the circumstances of their time. This is our peculiar method of work. All the modern reformers take to European destructive reformation, which will never do good to anyone and never did. Only once was a modern reformer mostly constructive, and that one was Raja Ram Mohan Ray. The progress of the Hindu race has been towards the realisation of the Vedantic ideals. All history of Indian life is the struggle for the realisation of the ideal of the Vedanta through good or bad fortune.

Whenever there was any reforming sect or religion which rejected the Vedantic ideal, it was smashed into nothing."

"What is your programme of work here?"

"I want to start two institutions, one in Madras and one in Calcutta, to carry out my plan; and that plan briefly is to bring the Vedantic ideals into the everyday practical life of the saint or the sinner, of the sage or the ignoramus, of the Brahmin or the Pariah."

Our representative here put to him a few questions relative to Indian politics; but before the Swami could attempt anything like an answer, the train steamed up to the Egmore platform, and the only hurried remark that fell from the Swami was that he was dead against all political entanglements of Indian and European problems. The interview then terminated.

The Missionary Work Of The First Hindu

Sannyasin To The West And His Plan Of Regeneration Of India

(Madras Times, February, 1897)

For the past few weeks, the Hindu public of Madras have been most eagerly expecting the arrival of Swami Vivekananda, the great Hindu monk of world-wide fame. At the present moment his name is on everybody's lips. In the school, in the college, in the High Court, on the marina, and in the streets and bazars of Madras, hundreds of inquisitive spirits may be seen asking when the Swami will be coming. Large numbers of students from the mofussil, who have come up for the University examinations are staying here, awaiting the Swami, and increasing their hostelry bills, despite the urgent call of their parents to return home immediately. In a few days the Swami will be in our midst. From the nature of the receptions received elsewhere in this Presidency, from the preparations being made here, from the triumphal arches erected at Castle Kernan, where the "Prophet" is to be lodged at the cost of the Hindu public, and from the interest taken in the movement by the leading Hindu gentlemen of this city, like the Hon'ble Mr. Justice Subramaniya Iyer, there is no doubt that the Swami will have a grand reception. It was Madras that first recognised the superior merits of the Swami and equipped him for Chicago. Madras will now have again the honour of welcoming the undoubtedly great man who has done so much to raise the prestige of his motherland. Four year ago, when the Swami arrived here, he was practically an obscure individual. In an unknown bungalow at St. Thome he spent nearly two months, all along holding conversations on religious topics and teaching and instructing all comers who cared to listen to him. Even then a few educated young men with "a keener eye" predicted that there was something in the man, "a power", that would lift him above all others, that would pre-eminently enable him to be the leader of men. These young men, who were then despised as "misguided enthusiasts", "dreamy revivalists", have now the supreme satisfaction of seeing their Swami, as they love to call him, return to them with a great European and American fame. The mission of the Swami is essentially spiritual. He firmly believes that India, the motherland of spirituality, has a great future before her. He is sanguine that the West will more and more come to appreciate what he regards as the sublime truths of Vedanta. His great motto is "Help, and not Fight" "Assimilation, and not Destruction", "Harmony and Peace, and not Dissension". Whatever difference of opinion followers of other creeds may have with him, few will venture to deny that the Swami has done yeoman's service to his country in opening the eyes of the Western world to "the good in the Hindu". He will always be remembered as the first Hindu Sannyâsin who dared to cross the sea to carry to the West the message of what he believes in as a religious peace.

A representative of our paper interviewed the Swami Vivekananda, with a view to eliciting from him an account of the success of his mission in the West. The Swami very courteously received our representative and motioned him to a chair by his side. The Swami was dressed in yellow robes, was calm, serene, and dignified, and appeared inclined to answer any questions that might be put to him. We have given the Swami's words as taken down in shorthand by our representative.

"May I know a few particulars about your early life?" asked our representative.

The Swami said: "Even while I was a student at Calcutta, I was of a religious temperament. I was critical even at that time of my life, mere words would not satisfy me. Subsequently I met Ramakrishna Paramahamsa, with whom I lived for a long time and under whom I studied. After the death of my father I gave myself up to travelling in India and started a little monastery in Calcutta. During my travels, I came to Madras, where I received help from the Maharaja of Mysore and the Raja of Ramnad."

"What made Your Holiness carry the mission of Hinduism to Western countries?"

"I wanted to get experience. My idea as to the keynote of our national downfall is that we do not mix with other nations — that is the one and the sole cause. We never had opportunity to compare notes. We were Kupa-Mandukas (frogs in a well)."

"You have done a good deal of travelling in the West?"

"I have visited a good deal of Europe, including Germany and France, but England and America were the chief centres of my work. At first I found myself in a critical position, owing to the hostile attitude assumed against the people of this country by those who went there from India. I believe the Indian nation is by far the most moral and religious nation in the whole world, and it would be a blasphemy to compare the Hindus with any other nation. At first, many fell foul of me, manufactured huge lies against me by saying that I was a fraud, that I had a harem of wives and half a regiment of children. But my experience of these missionaries opened my eyes as to what they are capable of doing in the name of religion. Missionaries were nowhere in England. None came to fight me. Mr. Lund went over to America to abuse me behind my back, but people would not listen to him. I was very popular with them. When I came back to England, I thought this missionary would be at me, but the *Truth* silenced him. In England the social status is stricter than caste is in India. The English Church people are all gentlemen born, which many of the missionaries are not. They greatly sympathised with me. I think that about thirty English Church clergymen agree entirely with me on all points of religious discussion. I was agreeably surprised to find that the English clergymen, though they differed from me, did not abuse me behind my back and stab me in the dark. There is the benefit of caste and hereditary culture."

"What has been the measure of your success in the West?"

"A great number of people sympathised with me in America — much more than in England. Vituperation by the low-caste missionaries made my cause succeed better. I had no money, the people of India having given me my bare passage-money, which was spent in a very short time. I had to live just as here on the charity of individuals. The Americans are a very hospitable people. In America one-third of the people are Christians, but the rest have no religion, that is they do not belong to any of the sects, but amongst them are to be found the most spiritual persons. I think the work in England is sound. If I die tomorrow and cannot send any more Sannyasins, still the English work will go on. The Englishman is a very good man. He is taught from his childhood to suppress all his feelings. He is thickheaded, and is not so quick as the Frenchman or the American. He is immensely practical. The American people are too young to understand renunciation. England has enjoyed wealth and luxury for ages. Many people there are ready for renunciation. When I first lectured in England I had a little class of twenty or thirty, which was kept going when I left, and when I went back from America I could get an audience of one thousand. In America I could get a much bigger one, as I spent three years in America and only one year in England. I have two Sannyasins — one in England and one in America, and I intend sending Sannyasins to other countries.

"English people are tremendous workers. Give them an idea, and you may be sure that that idea is not going to be lost, provided they catch it. People here have given up the Vedas, and all your philosophy is in the kitchen. The religion of India at present is 'Don't-touchism' — that is a religion which the English people will never accept. The thoughts of our forefathers and the wonderful life-giving principles that they discovered, every nation will take. The biggest guns of the English Church told me that I was putting Vedantism into the Bible. The present Hinduism is a degradation. There is no book on philosophy, written today, in which something of our Vedantism is not touched upon — even the works of Herbert Spencer contain it. The philosophy of the age is Advaitism, everybody talks of it; only in Europe, they try to be original. They talk of Hindus with contempt, but at the same time swallow the truths given out by the Hindus. Professor Max Müller is a perfect Vedantist, and has done splendid work in Vedantism. He believes in re-incarnation."

"What do you intend doing for the regeneration of India?"

"I consider that the great national sin is the neglect of the masses, and that is one of the causes of our downfall. No amount of politics would be of any avail until the masses in India are once more well educated, well fed, and well cared for. They pay for our education, they build our temples, but in return they get kicks. They are practically our slaves. If we want to regenerate India, we must work for them. I want to start two central institutions at first — one at Madras and the other at Calcutta — for training young men as preachers. I have funds for starting the Calcutta one. English people will find funds for my purpose.

"My faith is in the younger generation, the modern generation, out of them will come my workers. They will work out the whole problem, like lions. I have formulated the idea and have given my life to it. If I do not achieve success, some better one will come after me to work it out, and I shall be content to struggle. The one problem you have is to give to the masses their rights. You have the greatest religion which the world ever saw, and you feed the masses with stuff and nonsense. You have the perennial fountain flowing, and you give them ditch-water. Your Madras graduate would not touch a low-caste man, but is ready to get out of him the money for his education. I want to start at first these two institutions for educating missionaries to be both spiritual and secular instructors to our masses. They will spread from centre to centre, until we have covered the whole of India. The great thing is to have faith in oneself, even before faith in God; but the difficulty seems to be that we are losing faith in ourselves day by day. That is my objection against the reformers. The orthodox have more faith and more strength in themselves, in spite of their crudeness; but the reformers simply play into the hands of Europeans and pander to their vanity. Our masses are gods as compared with those of other countries. This is the only country where poverty is not a crime. They are mentally and physically handsome; but we hated and hated them till they have lost faith in themselves. They think they are born slaves. Give them their rights, and let them stand on their rights. This is the glory of the American civilization. Compare the Irishman with knees bent, half-starved, with a little stick and bundle of clothes, just arrived from the ship, with what he is, after a few months' stay in America. He walks boldly and bravely. He has come from a country where he was a slave to a country where he is a brother.

"Believe that the soul is immortal, infinite and all-powerful. My idea of education is personal contact with the teacher - Gurugriha-Vâsa. Without the personal life of a teacher there would be no education. Take your Universities. What have they done during the fifty years of their existences. They have not produced one original man. They are merely an examining body. The idea of the sacrifice for the common weal is not yet developed in our nation."

"What do you think of Mrs. Besant and Theosophy?"

"Mrs. Besant is a very good woman. I lectured at her Lodge in London. I do not know personally much about her. Her knowledge of our religion is very limited; she picks up scraps here and there; she never had time to study it thoroughly. That she is one of the most sincere of women, her greatest enemy will concede. She is considered the best speaker in England. She is a Sannyâsini. But I do not believe in Mahâtmâs and Kuthumis. Let her give up her connection with the Theosophical Society, stand on her own footing, and preach what she thinks right."

Speaking of social reforms, the Swami expressed himself about widow-marriage thus: "I have yet to see a nation whose fate is determined by the number of husbands their widows get."

Knowing as he did that several persons were waiting downstairs to have an interview with the Swami, our representative withdrew, thanking the Swami for the kindness with which he had consented to the journalistic torture.

The Swami, it may be remarked, is accompanied by Mr. and Mrs. J. H. Sevier, Mr. T. G. Harrison, a Buddhist gentleman of Colombo, and Mr. J. J. Goodwin. It appears that Mr. and Mrs. Sevier accompany the Swami with a view to settling in the Himalayas, where they intend building a residence for the Western disciples of the Swami, who may have an inclination to reside in India. For twenty years, Mr. and Mrs. Sevier had followed no particular religion, finding satisfaction in none of those that were preached; but on listening to a course of lectures by the Swami, they professed to have found a religion that satisfied their heart and intellect. Since then they have accompanied the Swami through Switzerland, Germany, and Italy, and now to India. Mr. Goodwin, a journalist in England, became a disciple of the Swami fourteen months ago, when he first met him at New York. He gave up his journalism and devotes himself to attending the Swami and taking down his lectures in shorthand. He is in every sense a true "disciple", saying that he hopes to be with the Swami till his death.

Reawakening Of Hinduism
On A National Basis

(Prabuddha Bharata, September, 1898)

In an interview which a representative of *Prabuddha Bharata* had recently with the Swami Vivekananda, that great Teacher was asked: "What do you consider the distinguishing feature of your movement, Swamiji?"

"Aggression," said the Swami promptly, "aggression in a religious sense only. Other sects and parties have carried spirituality all over India, but since the days of Buddha we have been the first to break bounds and try to flood the world with missionary zeal."

"And what do you consider to be the function of your movement as regards India?'

"To find the common bases of Hinduism and awaken the national consciousness to them. At present there are three parties in India included under the term 'Hindu' — the orthodox, the reforming sects of the Mohammedan period, and the reforming sects of the present time. Hindus from North to South are only agreed on one point, viz. on not eating beef."

"Not in a common love for the Vedas?"

"Certainly not. That is just what we want to reawaken. India has not yet assimilated the work of Buddha. She is hypnotised by his voice, not made alive by it."

"In what way do you see this importance of Buddhism in India today?"

"It is obvious and overwhelming. You see India never loses anything; only she takes time to turn everything into bone and muscle. Buddha dealt a blow at animal sacrifice from which India has never recovered; and Buddha said, 'Kill no cows', and cow-killing is an impossibility with us."

"With which of the three parties you name do you identify yourself, Swamiji?"

"With all of them. We are orthodox Hindus," said the Swami, "but", he added suddenly with great earnestness and emphasis, "we refuse entirely to identify ourselves with 'Don't-touchism'. That is not Hinduism: it is in none of our books; it is an unorthodox superstition which has interfered with national efficiency all along the line."

"Then what you really desire is national efficiency?"

"Certainly. Can you adduce any reason why India should lie in the ebb-tide of the Aryan nations? Is she inferior in intellect? Is she inferior in dexterity? Can you look at her art, at her mathematics, at her philosophy, and answer 'yes'? All that is needed is that she should de-hypnotise herself and wake up from her age-long sleep to take her true rank in the hierarchy of nations."

"But India has always had her deep inner life. Are you not afraid, Swamiji, that in attempting to make her active you may take from her, her one great treasure?"

"Not at all. The history of the past has gone to develop the inner life of India and the activity (i.e. the outer life) of the West. Hitherto these have been divergent. The time has now come for them to unite. Ramakrishna Paramahamsa was alive to the depths of being, yet on the outer plane who was more active? This is the secret. Let your life be as deep as the ocean, but let it also be as wide as the sky.

"It is a curious thing", continued the Swami, "that the inner life is often most profoundly developed where the outer conditions are most cramping and limiting. But this is an accidental — not an essential — association, and if we set ourselves right here in India, the world will be 'tightened'. For are we not all one?"

"Your last remarks, Swamiji, raise another question. In what sense is Shri Ramakrishna a part of this awakened Hinduism?"

"That is not for me to determine", said the Swami. "I have never preached personalities. My own life is guided by the enthusiasm of this great soul; but others will decide for themselves how far they share in this attitude. Inspiration is not filtered out to the world through one channel, however great. Each generation should be inspired afresh. Are we not all God?"

"Thank you. I have only one question more to ask you. You have defined the attitude and function of your movement with regard to your own people. Could you in the same way characterise your methods of action as a whole?"

"Our method", said the Swami, "is very easily described. It simply consists in reasserting the national life. Buddha preached *renunciation*. India heard, and yet in six centuries she reached heir greatest height. The secret lies there. The national ideals of India are RENUNCIATION and SERVICE. Intensify her in those channels, and the rest will take care of itself. The banner of the spiritual cannot be raised too high in this country. In it alone is salvation.

On Indian Women — Their Past, Present And Future

(Prabuddha Bharata, December, 1898)

It was early one Sunday morning, writes our representative, in a beautiful Himalayan valley, that I was at last able to carry out the order of the Editor, and call on the Swami Vivekananda, to ascertain something of his views on the position and prospects of Indian Women.

"Let us go for a walk", said the Swami, when I had announced my errand, and we set out at once amongst some of the most lovely scenery in the world.

By sunny and shady ways we went, through quiet villages, amongst playing children and across the golden cornfields. Here the tall trees seemed to pierce the blue above, and there a group of peasant girls stooped, sickle in hand, to cut and carry off the plume-tipped stalks of maize-straw for the winter stores. Now the road led into an apple orchard, where great heaps of crimson fruit lay under the trees for sorting, and again we were out in the open, facing the snows that rose in august beauty above the white clouds against the sky.

At last my companion broke the silence. "The Aryan and Semitic ideals of woman", he said, "have always been diametrically opposed. Amongst the Semites the presence of woman is considered dangerous to devotion, and she may not perform any religious function, even such as the killing of a bird for food: according to the Aryan a man cannot perform a religious action without a wife."

"But Swamiji!" said I — startled at an assertion so sweeping and so unexpected — "is Hinduism not an Aryan faith?"

"Modern Hinduism", said the Swami quietly, "is largely Paurânika, that is, post-Buddhistic in origin. Dayânanda Saraswati pointed out that though a wife is absolutely necessary in the Sacrifice of the domestic fire, which is a Vedic rite, she may not touch the Shâlagrâma Shilâ, or the household-idol, because that dates from the later period of the Purânas."

"And so you consider the inequality of woman amongst us as entirely due to the influence of Buddhism?"

"Where it exists, certainly," said the Swami, "but we should not allow the sudden influx of European criticism and our consequent sense of contrast to make us acquiesce too readily in this notion of the inequality of our women. Circumstances have forced upon us, for many centuries, the woman's need of protection. This, and not her inferiority, is the true reading of our customs."

"Are you then entirely satisfied with the position of women amongst us, Swamiji?"

"By no means," said the Swami, "but our right of interference is limited entirely to giving education. Women must be put in a position to solve their own problems in their own way. No one can or ought to do this for them. And our Indian women are as capable of doing it as any in the world."

"How do you account for the evil influence which you attribute to Buddhism?"

"It came only with the decay of the faith", said the Swami. "Every movement triumphs by dint of some unusual characteristic, and when it falls, that point of pride becomes its chief element of weakness. The Lord Buddha — greatest of men — was a marvellous organiser and carried the world by this means. But his religion was the religion of a monastic order. It had, therefore, the evil effect of making the very robe of the monk honoured. He also introduced for the first time the community life of religious houses and thereby necessarily made women inferior to men, since the great abbesses could take no important step without the advice of certain abbots. It ensured its immediate object, the solidarity of the faith, you see, only its far-reaching effects are to be deplored."

"But Sannyâsa is recognised in the Vedas!"

"Of course it is, but without making any distinction between men and women. Do you remember how Yâjnavalkya was questioned at the Court of King Janaka? His principal examiner was Vâchaknavi, the maiden orator — Brahmavâdini, as the word of the day was. 'Like two shining arrows in the hand of the skilled archer', she says, 'are my questions.' Her sex is not even commented upon. Again, could anything be more complete than the equality of boys and girls in our old forest universities? Read our Sanskrit dramas — read the story of Shakuntala, and see if Tennyson's 'Princess' has anything to teach us! "

"You have a wonderful way of revealing the glories of our past, Swamiji!"

"Perhaps, because I have seen both sides of the world," said the Swami gently, "and I know that the race that produced Sitâ — even if it only dreamt of her — has a reverence for woman that is unmatched on the earth. There is many a burden bound with legal tightness on the shoulders of Western women that is utterly unknown to ours. We have our wrongs and our exceptions certainly, but so have they. We must never forget that all over the globe the general effort is to express love and tenderness and uprightness, and that national customs are only the nearest vehicles of this expression. With regard to the domestic virtues I have no hesitation in saying that our Indian methods have in many ways the advantage over all others."

"Then have our women any problems at all, Swamiji?"

"Of course, they have many and grave problems, but none that are not to be solved by that magic word 'education'. The true education, however, is not yet conceived of amongst us."

"And how would you define that?"

"I never define anything", said the Swami, smiling. "Still, it may be described as a development of faculty, not an accumulation of words, or as a training of individuals to will rightly and efficiently. So shall we bring to the need of India great fearless women — women worthy to continue the traditions of Sanghamittâ, Lilâ, Ahalyâ Bâi, and Mirâ Bâi — women fit to be mothers of heroes, because they are pure and selfless, strong with the strength that comes of touching the feet of God."

"So you consider that there should be a religious element in education, Swamiji?"

"I look upon religion as the innermost core of education", said the Swami solemnly. "Mind, I do not mean my own, or any one else's opinion about religion. I think the teacher should take the pupil's starting-point in this, as in other respects, and enable her to develop along her own line of least resistance."

"But surely the religious exaltation of Brahmacharya, by taking the highest place from the mother and wife and giving it to those who evade those relations, is a direct blow dealt at woman?"

"You should remember", said the Swami, "that if religion exalts Brahmacharya for woman, it does exactly the same for man Moreover, your question shows a certain confusion in your own mind. Hinduism indicates one duty, only one, for the human soul. It is to seek to realise the permanent amidst the evanescent. No one presumes to point out any one way in which this may be done. Marriage or non-marriage, good or evil, learning or ignorance, any of these is justified, if it leads to the goal. In this respect lies the great contrast between it and Buddhism, for the latter's outstanding direction is to realise the impermanence of the external, which, broadly speaking, can only be done in one way. Do you recall the story of the young Yogi in the Mahâbhârata who prided himself on his psychic powers by burning the bodies of a crow and crane by his intense will, produced by anger? Do you remember that the young saint went into the town and found first a wife nursing her sick husband and then the butcher Dharma-Vyâdha, both of whom had obtained enlightenment in the path of common faithfulness and duty?"

"And so what would you say, Swamiji, to the women of this country?

"Why, to the women of this country." said the Swami, "I would say exactly what I say to the men. Believe in India and in our Indian faith. Be strong and hopeful and unashamed, and remember that with something to take, Hindus have immeasurably more to give than any other people in the world."

On The Bounds Of Hinduism

(Prabuddha Bharata, April, 1899)

Having been directed by the Editor, writes our representative, to interview Swami Vivekananda on the question of converts to Hinduism, I found an opportunity one evening on the roof of a Ganga houseboat. It was after nightfall, and we had stopped at the embankment of the Ramakrishna Math, and there the Swami came down to speak with me.

Time and place were alike delightful. Overhead the stars, and around — the rolling Ganga; and on one side stood the dimly lighted building, with its background of palms and lofty shade-trees.

"I want to see you, Swami", I began, "on this matter of receiving back into Hinduism those who have been perverted from it. Is it your opinion that they should be received?"

"Certainly," said the Swami, "they can and ought to be taken."

He sat gravely for a moment, thinking, and then resumed. "Besides," he said, "we shall otherwise decrease in numbers. When the Mohammedans first came, we are said — I think on the authority of Ferishta, the oldest Mohammedan historian — to have been six hundred millions of Hindus. Now we are about two hundred millions. And then every man going out of the Hindu pale is not only a man less, but an enemy the more.

"Again, the vast majority of Hindu perverts to Islam and Christianity are perverts by the sword, or the descendants of these. It would be obviously unfair to subject these to disabilities of any kind. As to the case of born aliens, did you say? Why, born aliens have been converted in the past by crowds, and the process is still going on.

"In my own opinion, this statement not only applies to aboriginal tribes, to outlying nations, and to almost all our conquerors before the Mohammedan conquest, but also in the Purânas. I hold that they have been aliens thus adopted.

"Ceremonies of expiation are no doubt suitable in the case of willing converts, returning to their Mother-Church, as it were; but on those who were alienated by conquest — as in Kashmir and Nepal — or on strangers wishing to join us, no penance should be imposed."

"But of what caste would these people be, Swamiji?" I ventured to ask. "They must have some, or they can never be assimilated into the great body of Hindus. Where shall we look for their rightful place?"

"Returning converts", said the Swami quietly, "will gain their own castes, of course. And new people will make theirs. You will remember," he added, "that this has already been done in the case of Vaishnavism. Converts from different castes and aliens were all able to combine under that flag and form a caste by themselves — and a very respectable one too. From Râmânuja down to Chaitanya of Bengal, all great Vaishnava Teachers have done the same."

"And where should these new people expect to marry?" I asked.

"Amongst themselves, as they do now", said the Swami quietly.

"Then as to names," I enquired, "I suppose aliens and perverts who have adopted non-Hindu names should be named newly. Would you give them caste-names, or what?"

"Certainly," said the Swami, thoughtfully, "there is a great deal in a name!" and on this question he would say no more.

But my next enquiry drew blood. "Would you leave these new-comers, Swamiji, to choose their own form of religious belief out of many-visaged Hinduism, or would you chalk out a religion for them?"

"Can you ask that?" he said. "They will choose for themselves. For unless a man chooses for himself, the very spirit of Hinduism is destroyed. The essence of our Faith consists simply in this freedom of the Ishta."

I thought the utterance a weighty one, for the man before me has spent more years than any one else living I fancy, in studying the common bases of Hinduism in a scientific and sympathetic spirit — and the freedom of the Ishta is obviously a principle big enough to accommodate the world.

But the talk passed to other matters, and then with a cordial good night this great teacher of religion lifted his lantern and went back into the monastery, while I by the pathless paths of the Ganga, in and out amongst her crafts of many sizes, made the best of my way back to my Calcutta home.

www.ingramcontent.com/pod-product-compliance
Lightning Source LLC
LaVergne TN
LVHW091134180726
843490LV00008B/2969